SWIMMING LESSONS

NATURE'S MOTHERS

WYLAND.

Also by Wyland with Steve Creech

Hold Your Water! 68 Things You Need to Know to Keep Our Planet Blue

SWIMMING LESSONS
NATURE'S MOTHERS

SEA LIONS

Fine-Art Nature Photography by Wyland
Written by STEVE CREECH

Andrews McMeel
Publishing, LLC
Kansas City

07 08 09 10 11 SDB 10 9 8 7 6 5 4 3 2 1

ISBN-13: 978-0-7407-6081-5
ISBN-10: 0-7407-6081-5

Library of Congress Control Number: 2006937279

www.andrewsmcmeel.com

www.wyland.com

ATTENTION: SCHOOLS AND BUSINESSES

Andrews McMeel books are available at quantity discounts with bulk purchase for educational, business, or sales promotional use. For information, please write to: Special Sales Department, Andrews McMeel Publishing, LLC, 4520 Main Street, Kansas City, Missouri 64111.

The bond in the animal kingdom is often a reflection of our own. I've seen mothers in the wild risk everything to see their children survive. I've seen them give, nurture, and teach. I've seen them on the brink of starvation so that their offspring might eat. Call it instinct if you want. But if something looks like love, it must certainly be.

—Wyland

Acknowledgments

Most of the sea lions in this book were photographed in Baja California Sur. Thanks to the work of groups like the International Community Foundation, the Nature Conservancy, and the Fund for the Protected Areas in Southern Baja California, the rocky islands in this region remain as unspoiled as they have been for centuries. We also thank the Pacific Mammal Research Center for their consulting expertise and for their work in saving and rehabilitating these remarkable animals. As always, a heartfelt thanks to Dorothy O'Brien at Andrews McMeel Publishing and her team; Gregg Hamby, our talented graphic designer; Karla Kipp for her production work; and Angela Needham, Steve Creech, and Deana Duffek for their commitment to quality.

Introduction

At this point in my life, I'm proud to say I have encountered some of the greatest wonders in nature. Great whales. Giant mantas. Vast seas, magnificent lakes, and powerful rivers. Many of these things I could once only imagine. Now, having seen many of them, I am still filled with awe. More and more, I find myself turning my camera lens toward the cycle of life in nature. As I see a mother and pup in the wild, I ask myself many questions: What conditions will they encounter over the next year? Will they face predators? Will the pup have enough food to reach its amazing potential? What impact are we, as humans, having on its world?

To put together a photographic book about sea lion mothers is a great honor for me. I am a humble visitor to these places, an alien looking out through a fish-eye camera lens, searching for some indescribable truth. I can only thank these animals for allowing me the privilege of spending time with them, of discovering how they live and the challenges they face. For me, it's weeks in chilly water, then a happy return to the refuge of my boat. For them, the story is entirely different. There are no guarantees in their lives. There is only the struggle to raise their offspring—and to survive.

—Wyland

They sleep on rocky beds, spend their lives wearing the same coat, and often have to make do with sardines, night after night. But sea lion mothers know it's all in a day's work—and they do it gladly to raise healthy pups.

Sometimes that means keeping an eye out for trouble, while others sleep.

Late hours.

And always looking for ways to put food on the table.

If that weren't enough, there always seems to be a male around, barking and snorting.

Sea lion mothers do their share of barking, too. But it's not to hear their own voice. A mother teaches her pup the sound of her voice—a sound imprint—so the pup can identify her from all the other mothers in the days ahead.

And the pups?

They bark right back—so Mother learns their voice, as well.

At birth, a healthy pup is well over a foot long.

In less than an hour, it can groom itself, scratch, and walk.

And, like its mother, it loves sunbathing.

Sometimes a mother has to remind her pup that it has to "walk" before it can swim.

When the barking is done, mothers *always* remember to forgive.

The pup has learned its first lessons. Now it is ready to see what else lies on the horizon.

With the pups safe and secure, the mothers go "grocery" shopping.

But a mother's absence can seem like an eternity. So the pups wait . . .

and wait . . .

and wait.

Mother's return makes everybody happy.

Swimming lessons: the most important rite of passage in the sea lion world. Mothers lead, and pups follow. It's a sea lion version of "monkey see, monkey do."

Mother rolls and dips with a thrust of her large, winglike fore flippers.

Her pup can only hope one day to match her grace and agility.

The training takes long days.

Months pass.

Soon, the clumsy little pup becomes a thing of wonder and strikes off on its own.

As years pass, the male pups become strong and powerful.

Females become expert hunters.

They are faster, smarter, and tougher than ever.

They dive the darkest depths . . .

swim with incredible speed . . .

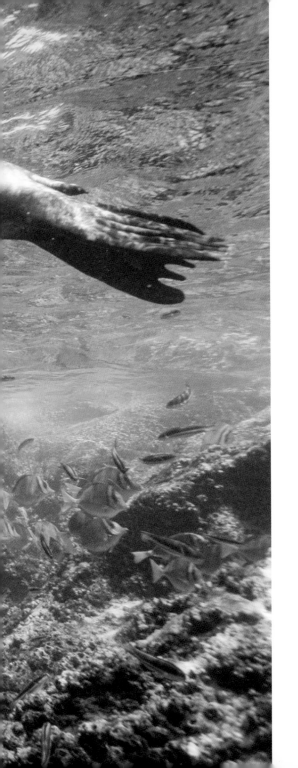

and maneuver with awe-inspiring agility.

For some it has been years since those first lessons.

But the "pups" persevere. They have survived the perils of harsh environments.

They have seen many wonders.

But they will never forget the lessons their mothers taught them.

And perhaps one day they will pass along those lessons to their own pups.

About Wyland

Marine life artist Wyland has earned distinction as one of America's most unique creative influences, and is a leading advocate for marine resource conservation. An accomplished painter, sculptor, photographer, and Scuba diver, he has traveled the farthest reaches of the globe for more than twenty-five years, capturing the raw power and beauty of the undersea universe.

His nonprofit Wyland Foundation has supported numerous conservation programs since 1993, including Wyland's monumental Whaling Wall mural project, an epic series of more than ninety-four life-size marine life murals that spans twelve countries on four continents, and is viewed by an estimated one billion people every year. The artist's efforts have been recognized by the United Nations, the Sierra Club, and private and public institutions throughout the world.

Steve Creech has coauthored several books with Wyland, including *Chicken Soup for the Ocean Lover's Soul* and *Hold Your Water: 68 Things You Need to Know to Keep Our Planet Blue.*

About the Wyland Foundation

The Wyland Foundation is a 501c3 nonprofit organization that inspires people to care about our oceans and related marine ecosystems. Founded in 1993 by marine life artist Wyland, the foundation encourages involvement in conservation through classroom education programs, community service, and art in public places. Together, Wyland and the Wyland Foundation have been responsible for more than ninety-four conservation-themed marine life murals in seventy cities in twelve countries around the world and has staged marine resources education and science tours in every state in the nation, including annual cleanup events on the East and West coasts and, most recently, a ten-state clean-water awareness tour throughout the Mississippi River watershed. The foundation's newest book, *Hold Your Water: 68 Things You Need to Know to Keep Our Planet Blue*, provides practical tips and insights for preserving our most precious resource.